Ambulances
on the Go

by Kerry Dinmont

BUMBA BOOKS™

LERNER PUBLICATIONS ◆ MINNEAPOLIS

Note to Educators:

Throughout this book, you'll find critical thinking questions. These can be used to engage young readers in thinking critically about the topic and in using the text and photos to do so.

Lerner Publications Company
A division of Lerner Publishing Group, Inc.
241 First Avenue North
Minneapolis, MN 55401 USA

For reading levels and more information, look up this title at www.lernerbooks.com.

Library of Congress Cataloging-in-Publication Data

The Cataloging-in-Publication Data for *Ambulances on the* Go is on file at the Library of Congress.
ISBN 978-1-5124-1448-6 (lib. bdg.)
ISBN 978-1-5124-1487-5 (pbk.)
ISBN 978-1-5124-1488-2 (EB pdf)

Manufactured in the United States of America
1 – VP – 7/15/16

LERNER
e
SOURCE

Expand learning beyond the printed book. Download free, complementary educational resources for this book from our website, www.lernerresource.com.

Table of Contents

Ambulances

Ambulances help people.

They take hurt and sick people

to the hospital.

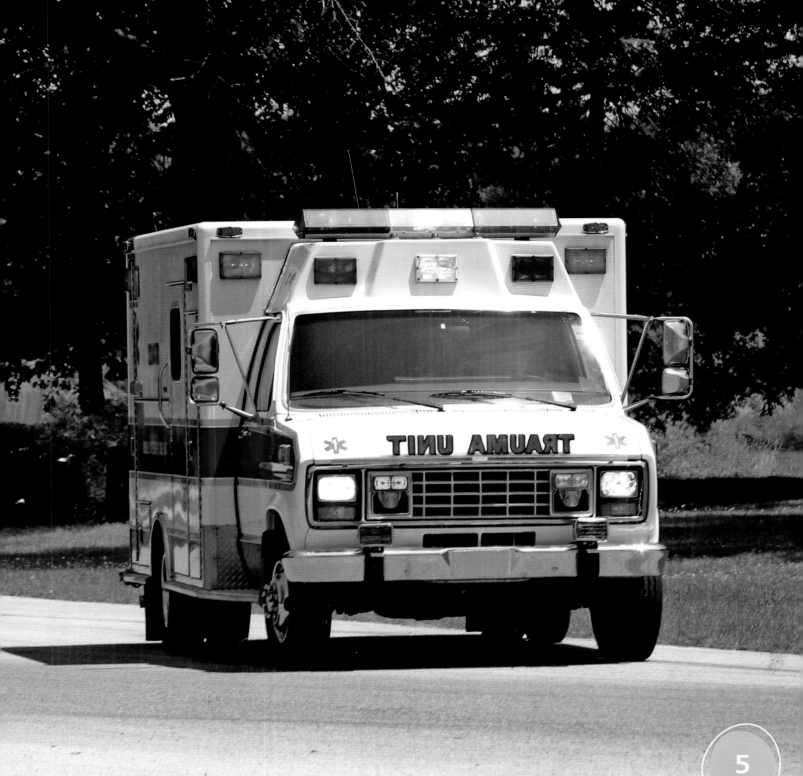

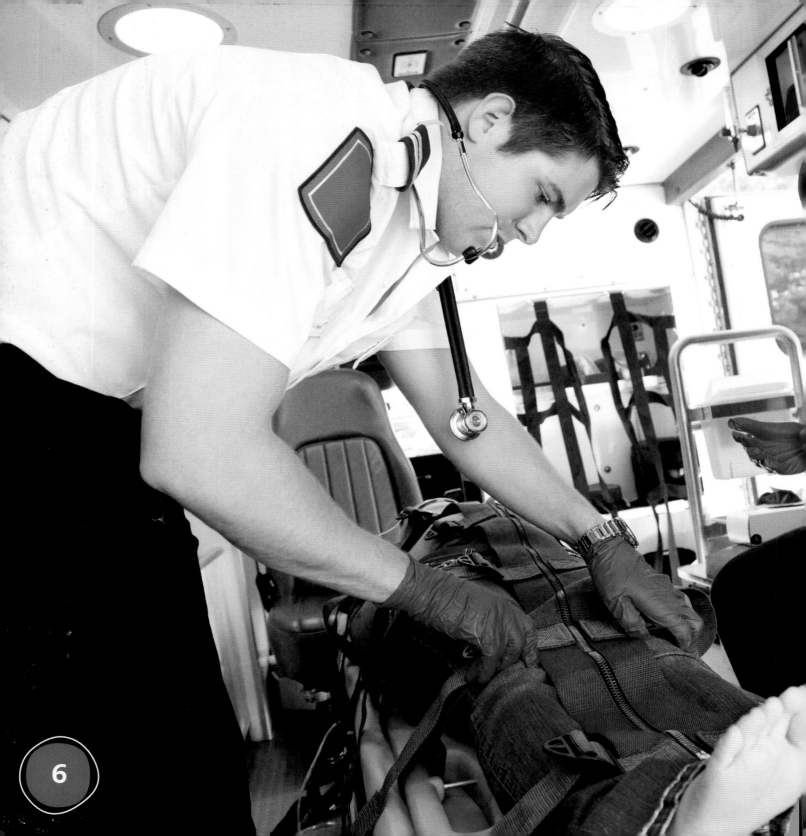

EMTs work in ambulances.
They are trained to help
people who are hurt.

The sirens sound.

Lights flash.

The ambulance drives fast.

It rushes to a hurt person.

Why do you think ambulances have sirens and lights?

A driver sits in front.

More EMTs sit in the back.

The back is a square room.

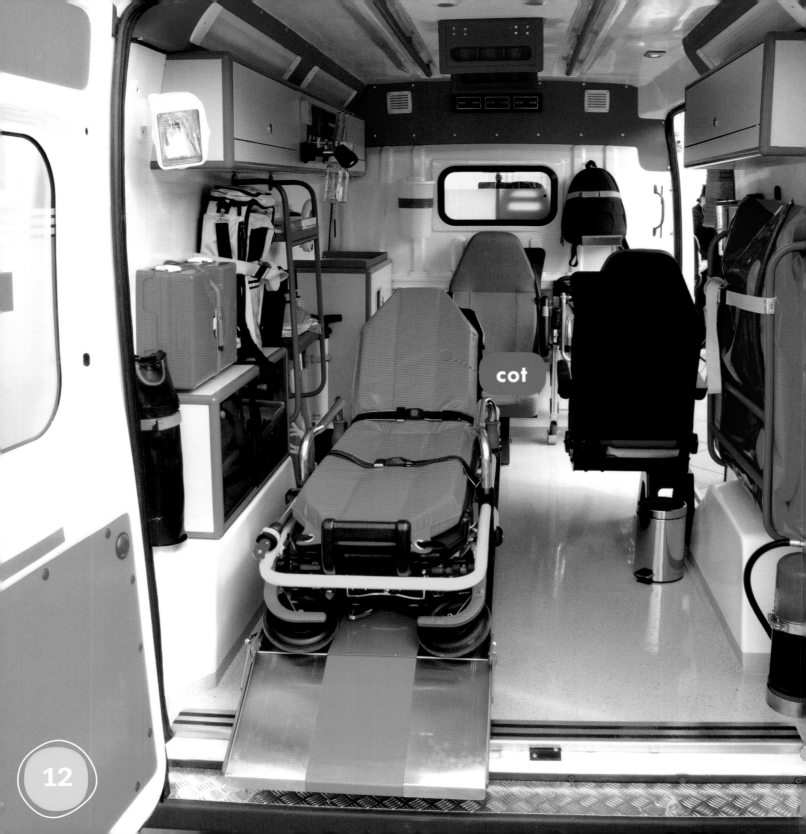

cot

An ambulance is wide.

It has room for a cot.

Why do you think ambulances have cots?

13

Ambulances hold many tools and machines. These tools keep very hurt people alive.

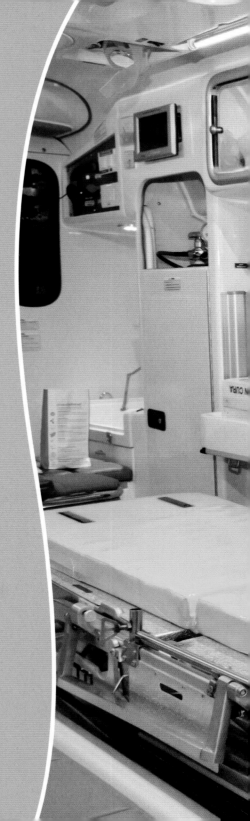

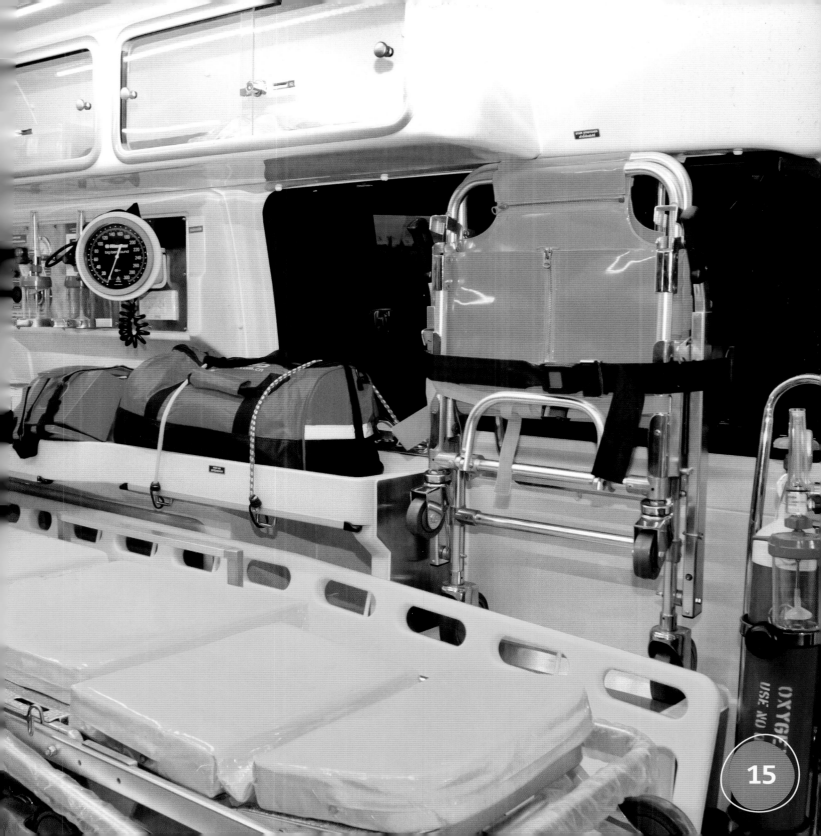

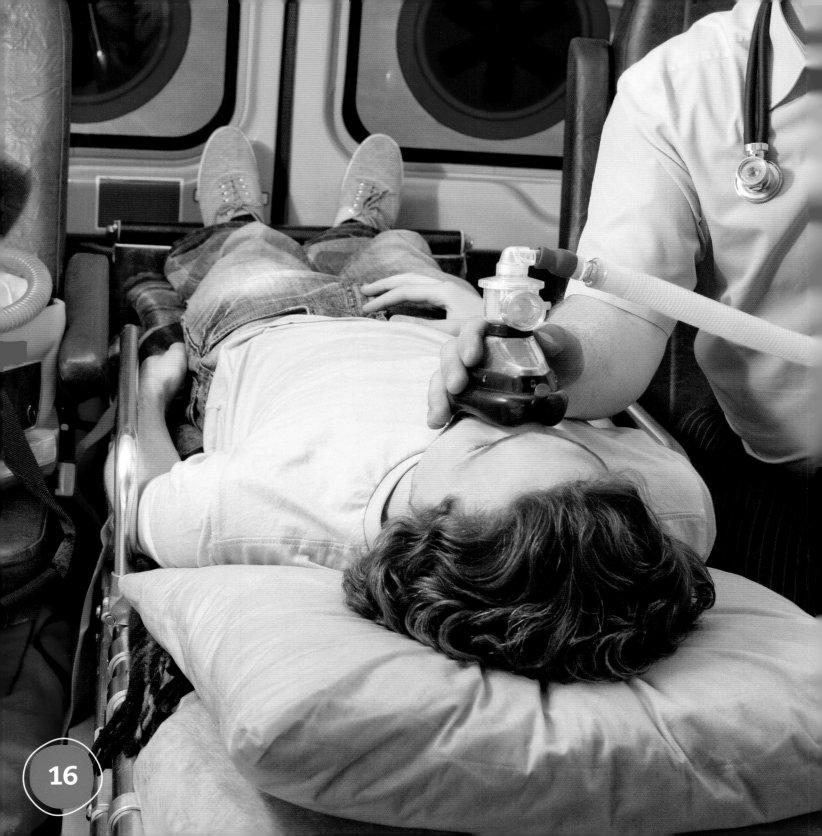

A patient lies in the back.

He needs a doctor.

An EMT makes him feel better

on the way to the hospital.

The ambulance races
to the hospital.
Other cars move when
they see the lights and
hear the sirens.

**Why should
cars move for
ambulances?**

Ambulances help save lives.

Do you want to work in one?

21

Parts of an Ambulance

lights

sirens

back

front

Picture Glossary

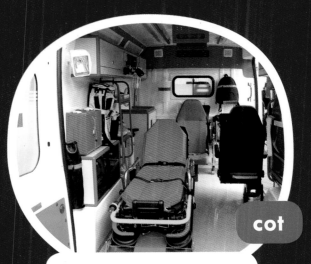

cot

a small bed that can be moved

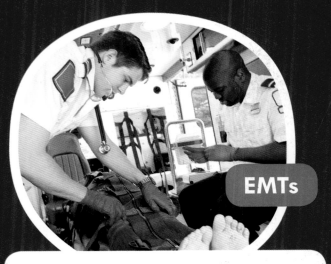

EMTs

people who are trained to help people who are hurt

lights

parts of the ambulance that flash and give off light

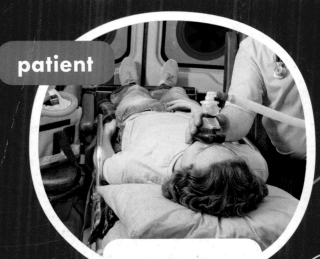

patient

a person who is hurt

Index

Read More

Graubart, Norman D. *Ambulances.* New York: PowerKids Press, 2015.

Hamilton Waxman, Laura. *Ambulances on the Move.* Minneapolis: Lerner Publications, 2011.

Riggs, Kate. *To the Rescue!* Mankato, MN: Creative Editions, 2015.

Photo Credits

The images in this book are used with the permission of: © HodagMedia/iStock.com/Thinkstock, p. 5; © Steve Debenport/iStock.com, pp. 6–7, 23 (top right); © Daniel Barnes/iStock.com, pp. 9, 23 (bottom left); © Tyler Olson/Shutterstock.com, p. 11; © thelefty/Shutterstock.com, pp. 12, 23 (top left); © My Life Graphic/Shutterstock.com, pp. 14–15; © Capifrutta/Shutterstock.com, p. 16, 23 (bottom right); © cleanfotos/Shutterstock.com, pp. 18–19; © Susan Chiang/iStock.com, p. 21; © heathernemec/iStock.com, p. 22.

Front Cover: © heathernemec/iStock.